THE
OCTOBER
BABY

By Noel Streatfeild and available from Headline

The January Baby

The February Baby

The March Baby

The April Baby

The May Baby

The June Baby

The July Baby

The August Baby

The September Baby

The October Baby

The November Baby

The December Baby

THE
October
BABY

★

Noel Streatfeild

First published in 1959
This edition published in 2023 by Headline Home
an imprint of Headline Publishing Group

1

Cataloguing in Publication Data is available from the British Library

Hardback ISBN 978 1 0354 0857 3
eISBN 978 1 0354 0858 0

Typeset in 14.75/15pt Centaur MT Pro by Jouve (UK), Milton Keynes

Printed and bound in Great Britain by Clays Ltd, Elcograf S.p.A.

HEADLINE PUBLISHING GROUP
An Hachette UK Company
Carmelite House
50 Victoria Embankment
London EC4Y 0DZ

www.headline.co.uk
www.hachette.co.uk

CONTENTS

THE October baby has arrived. Telephones have rung, letters and telegrams have passed on the good news. All the usual questions have been asked, 'Is it a boy or is it a girl?' 'Who does it look like?' 'What does it weigh?' And above all, 'How is she? Did she have a bad time?' And now the moment has arrived when visitors are allowed, and everyone is asking themselves 'What shall I take her?'

It is possible for the mother of an October baby to have too many chrysanthemums. Being at their best they are such a temptation in the flower shop windows, that it is easy to forget that others may have thought of chrysanthemums too. It is also easy to forget the nurse who has to put them in water. Chrysanthemums, whether they are those enormous ones with faces like leopards, the shaggy or the smooth types, or even the

button ones, are only suited to certain kinds of vases, and whether in a hospital, a nursing home, or at home, the supply can run out. It is interesting to speculate what is being thought by the nurse who says for the twelfth time in one afternoon 'Aren't they lovely!'

Fruit is a nice present, and if it is peaches or exotics, a popular one. But like chrysanthemums it is possible to have too

many grapes, especially if each bunch is bought in perfect condition for eating that day!

Clothes for baby are of course the right present. But so few of us are strong-minded enough to hold on to the baby clothes we have bought or made until the baby arrives; it is so tempting to post the parcel right away. Something for the mother to wear is obviously ideal too, but such presents cost money and so are not within the reach of all.

There was a time when having a baby meant lying in bed for a whole month. In those days obviously books must have been an ideal present, for the mother had so much time on her hands when she could read. Today, with so much less time spent in bed,

mothers seem to have no time at all, and so something that is intended for snack reading seems called for.

It was while visiting a mother and a new baby that the idea for this book was born. We had, as is usual on such occasions, talked

almost entirely about the baby, and suddenly I thought, I wish there was a book I could give her about nothing but babies born in this particular month.

Here then is the October Baby's book. It starts with a list of possible names. To many this will be useless, for the baby's names have been chosen months ago. But there are those who are still havering, or are bogged down in a welter of too many family names. The names suggested here all have some relation to October.

Even if you don't believe in the signs of the zodiac, it is fun to see what sort of person the stars suggest your child will grow up to be. But as well, for every day of the month, there is a list of the distinguished who were born on that day, and very surprising some of them are. Who would have guessed that writer of delicate English, Katherine Mansfield, would share a birthday with a dynamic soldier and statesman such as Eisenhower? Or stranger still, who could imagine that sixteenth century diarist and gardener, John Evelyn, was born under the same stars as Chiang Kai-shek? Maybe you will find those who could share your baby's birthday equally inexplicable.

NAMES
for the
OCTOBER
BABY

OCTOBER is the month when the trees are a glory of crimson and gold. *Aurea* and *Aurelia* for girls and *Aurelian* for a boy mean 'golden'. The girl's name *Flavia* means 'yellow'. *Rory Roy* and *Russell* are 'red', and *Murray* is 'dark red'. *Griffin* and *Griffith* are 'ruddy'.

'Then to gather nuts is pleasant'... only one sort of nut-tree seems to have given its name to humans, the Hazel, but from it come these other girls' names *Eileen*, *Evelina* and *Eveline*, and the boy's name *Evelyn*.

October is named October because for the Romans it was the eighth month in the year. *Octavia* for a girl and *Octavius* for a boy both mean 'eighth'.

October was called the Wine-month by the Saxons, so for those who respect wines today, a wine name though unusual would be charming. How about *Claret* or *Sherry* for a girl, and *Port* or *Burgundy* for a boy?

The birthstone for October is the opal. *Opal* is one of the jewel names for girls.

The special apostle assigned to October is

Simon (Zelotes). *Simon* and *Simeon* mean 'obedient'. The virtues are not usually the meaning of boys' names, but here are a selection that have virtuous meanings. *Clement* means 'merciful', and *Curtis* 'courteous'. *Darby* and *Dermot* 'free from envy', *Goddard* 'pious'. *Hilary* and *Tate* 'cheerful'. *Horace* and *Horatio* 'punctual'. *Innocent* 'harmless'. *Jocelin, Jocelyn* and *Joscelin* 'merry'. *Philemon* 'loving', and *Terence* 'smooth' (a doubtful quality).

The 1st of October is the day of the Blessed Christopher Buxton. *Christopher* means 'Christ-bearing'.

St Thomas of Hereford has his day on the 3rd of October. *Thomas* means 'twin'.

The 4th of October is the day of St Francis of Assisi. *Francis* means 'free', as does *Frank*. The girls' versions of the name are *Frances, Francesca* and *Fanny*.

St Kenneth's Day is the 11th of October. *Kenneth* means 'handsome', and *Kevin* 'handsome child'.

The 12th of October is St Edwin's Day. *Edwin* means 'rich friend'.

The 13th of October belongs to Edward the Confessor. *Edward* means 'rich ward'.

The 15th of October is the day of St Teresa of Avila. *Teresa* means 'reaper'.

St Bertrand's Day is the 16th of October. *Bertrand* means 'bright raven'.

St Luke the Evangelist has his day on the 18th of October, the name means merely 'from Lucania'. The girl's name *Lucasta* comes from the same source.

The Blessed Philip Howard's Day is the 19th of October. *Philip* means 'horse lover'; the girl's version is *Philippa.*

The 20th of October is the day of St Irene. *Irene* means 'peace'.

St Ursula's Day is the 21st of October. *Ursula* means 'little bear'.

The 25th of October is the day of St Crispin. *Crispin* means 'curled'.

St Vincent's Day is the 27th of October. *Vincent* means 'conquering'.

The 30th of October is the day of the Blessed Dorothy of Montau. *Dorothy* means 'gift of God', as do *Dorothea* and *Theodora.* Close to this in meaning is *Ann,* which means 'He (God) has favoured me'. *Ann* has many different forms: *Anita, Anna, Anne, Annette, Annie, Hannah, Nan, Nancy, Nanette* or *Nina.*

Elisabeth, which means 'God hath sworn', has even more versions: they are *Bella, Belle, Beth, Betty, Elise, Eliza, Elizabeth, Elspah, Elsie, Elspeth, Elspie, Isabel, Isabella, Lisa, Lise* or *Lisette. Jessica* is another name with much the same meaning – 'God is looking'. For those who fancy something really original, how about *Mehetabel* which means 'benefited by God'?

'Brown October brings the pheasant'; there are quite a lot of brown names: *Donoghue*

'brown chieftain', *Duncan* 'brown warrior', *Duff* and *Nigel* which both mean 'dark', and *Dhugal, Dowal, Dougal* and *Dugald*, which mean 'dark stranger'. For girls *Leila, Lela* and *Lila* mean 'darkness'. But for a truly October name for a little girl which is seldom used, how about *Pheasant*?

If your baby is a son and born on Hallowe'en something rather fanciful in the way of a name seems indicated. All sorts of spirits are supposed to be abroad, including Pan, so how about *Dobie* or *Hunter*?

Finally, because the autumn term is the beginning of the educational year, here are two alphabets of names for you to study, one for a girl and the other for a boy.

Ava	*Gale*	*Audie*	*Gary*
Brenda	*Hedy*	*Burt*	*Hurd*
Cyd	*Ingrid*	*Cary*	*Irving*
Debra	*Jarma*	*Dirk*	*Jule*
Edna	*Kim*	*Elvis*	*Kirk*
Faye	*Lana*	*Farley*	*Lon*

Marsha	Trudy	Marlon	Trevor
Nydia	Una	Niles	Urban
Osa	Vanessa	Orson	Van
Petula	Wanda	Perry	Wayne
Queenie	Xenia	Quentin	Xeno
Ruth	Yorke	Rock	Yule
Shelley	Zita	Scott	Zachary

GIFTS
for the
OCTOBER
BABY

IF a godparent or other well-wisher would like to give the October baby a piece of jewellery, the right stone is the opal. This is supposed to be unlucky if worn by anyone not born in October, a legend which seems to have no bearing on truth. The opal is the emblem of hope, and the October baby who is given a piece of jewellery set with opals, will find it a talisman against diseases of the eyes, at least so Leonardus said in 1750 in *The Mirror of Stones*.

'(It) prevails against all the Diseases of the Eyes. It sharpens and strengthens the Sight. It cannot be improper to attribute to it so many Virtues, since it partakes of the Nature and Colour of so many Stones.'

The charming old custom of arranging

flowers in a bunch or vase so that it brings a message is almost forgotten today. But if your baby should receive a bunch of marigolds, persicaria and meadow saffron, it will mean a prediction (marigold) that your baby will have great powers of recovery (persicaria) and mirth (meadow saffron).

If your baby was born between the 1st and the 23rd of October read pages 24 and 25, but if between the 24th and the 31st skip to pages 26 and 27.

UNDER
WHAT STARS
WAS MY BABY
BORN?

LIBRA
The Scales
24th September–23rd October

SCORPIO
The Scorpion
24th October–22nd November

SAGITTARIUS
The Archer
23rd November–21st December

CAPRICORN
The Sea Goat
22nd December–20th January

AQUARIUS
The Water Bearer
21st January–19th February

PISCES
The Fishes
20th February–20th March

ARIES
The Ram
21st March–20th April

TAURUS
The Bull
21st April–21st May

GEMINI
The Twins
22nd May–21st June

CANCER
The Crab
22nd June–23rd July

LEO
The Lion
24th July–23rd August

VIRGO
The Virgin
24th August–23rd September

Libra — the Scales
24th September–23rd October

THE special characteristic of people born under Libra is intuition. They have great breadth of perception and not so much a lack of the power to reason as a lack of the necessity to do so, so thoroughly can they depend upon intuitive acuteness. Librans are refined and unassuming, demonstratively affectionate, and easily influenced by others. When in uncongenial surroundings they are more apt to look for solace within themselves than to muster the energy needed to change their circumstances. They lack physical strength too, though their bodies are likely to be of unusually harmonious proportions. Librans are disquieted by injustice and may find a career in combatting it. They have a ready weapon in their outstanding grace of elocution.

For the Libra Baby

Lucky to wear an opal.
Lucky stones are malachite, turquoise.
Lucky metal is copper.
The Libra baby's colour is green.
Lucky number is 6.
Luckiest day is Friday.

Scorpio — the Scorpion
24th October–22nd November

PEOPLE born under Scorpio have strong
and well-defined personalities. Passionate
and wilful, they are at the same time
reserved to the point of secretiveness. In them
love easily turns to jealousy and anger to
resentment. Their feelings are keen rather
than tender. Dignity in appearance and in
behaviour expresses their great self-esteem.
They select as friends only those to whom they
can extend some of this esteem, so their

friendships are few but correspondingly firm. In thinking they are detailed and persistent, and if their instinct for the physical organism inclines them to medicine as a profession, one would expect them to be outstanding in it.

For the Scorpio Baby

Lucky to wear garnet, bloodstone.
Lucky stone is flint.
Lucky metal is iron.
The Scorpio baby's colour is red.
Lucky number is 9.
Luckiest day is Tuesday.

BABIES BORN
ON
THE SAME DAY
AS
YOUR BABY

IS there any special good fortune in being born on one particular day? Is there any truth in a horoscope? Will babies born under Libra grow up like this, and those born under the sign of Scorpio grow up to be like that? Here is a list for you to help you make up your mind whether there is any truth in what the stars foretell.

1st   Henry III, 1207. August Henry Fitzroy, 3rd Duke of Grafton, 1735. George Colman, 1762.

2nd   Richard III, 1452. Elizabeth Montagu, 1720. Paul von Hindenburg, 1847. Marshal Foch, 1851. Mahatma Gandhi, 1869. Dame Myra Curtis, 1886. Graham Greene, 1904.

3rd   Marion Delorme, 1613. William Crawford Gorgas, 1854.

4th Mary Elizabeth Braddon, 1837. Richard Cromwell, 1626. Jean Francois Millet, 1814. Engelbert Dollfuss, 1892. Charles Heston, 1923.

5th Margaret, queen of Alexander III of Scotland, 1240. Mary of Modena, 1658. Jonathan Edwards, 1703. Denis Diderot, 1713. Horace Walpole, 4th Earl of Orford, 1717. Glynis Johns, 1923.

6th Emily, Duchess of Leinster, 1731. Louis Philippe I of France, 1773. Jenny Lind, 1820. Charles-Eduard Le Corbusier, 1887. Ethel Mannin, 1900. Mrs Barbara Anne Castle, 1911.

7th Archbishop Laud, 1573. Caroline Ann Southey, 1786. Niels Bohr, 1885. Sarah Churchill, 1916.

8th John Cowper Powys, 1872. Sir Alfred Munnings, 1878. Juan Domingo Perón, 1895. Prof. Marcus Oliphant, 1901. Ferenc Nagy, 1903. Sir Hugh Foot, 1907. Ron Randell, 1918.

9th Cervantes (baptized 9th October), 1547. Charles I of France, 1757. Dreyfus, 1859. Alastair Sim, 1900. Lord Hailsham, 1907. Edward, Duke of Kent, 1935.

10th   Jean Antoine Watteau, 1684. Henry Cavendish, 1731. Benjamin West, 1738. Giuseppe Verdi, 1813. Paul Kruger, 1825. Isabella II of Spain, 1830. Rufus Isaacs, Marquess of Reading, 1860. Fridtjof Nansen, 1861. Lord Nuffield, 1877. Helen Hayes, 1900.

11th   Sir Bernard Partridge, 1861. Mrs Eleanor Roosevelt, 1884.

12th   Edward VI, 1537. Helena Modjeska, 1840. Ramsay MacDonald, 1866. Vaughan Williams, 1872.

13th   Sophia, Electress of Hanover, 1630. Marshal Saxe, 1693. Ferdinand VII of Spain, 1784. Sir Geoffrey Vickers, 1894.

14th   James II, 1633. William Penn, 1644. George Grenville, 1712. Eamon de Valera, 1882. Katherine Mansfield, 1888. Dwight D. Eisenhower, 1890.

15th   Virgil, 70 B.C. Elizabeth Inchbald, 1753. Fanny Kelly, 1790. Nietzsche, 1844. Phyllis Neilson Terry, 1892. C. P. Snow, 1905.

16th   James II of Scotland, 1430. Oscar Wilde, 1856. Austen Chamberlain, 1863.

David Ben-Gurion, 1886. Eugene O'Neill, 1888.

17th   Saint-Simon, 1760. Lord Dalhousie, 1914. Arthur Miller, 1915. Rita Hayworth, 1919. Montgomery Clift, 1920.

18th   Pope Pius II, 1405. Prince Eugene of Savoy, 1663. Beau Nash, 1674. Peg Woffington, circa 1714. Thomas Love Peacock, 1785. Henri Bergson, 1859. Logan Pearsall Smith, 1865. Sidney G. Holland, 1893.

19th   Sir Thomas Browne, 1605. James Butler, Duke of Ormonde, 1610. Leigh Hunt, 1784.

20th   Sir Christopher Wren, 1632. Sophia Charlotte, Queen of Prussia, 1668. Lord Palmerston, 1784. Thomas Hughes, 1822. Rimbaud, 1854. Anna Neagle, 1904.

21st   Samuel Taylor Coleridge, 1772. Alphonse de Lamartine, 1790. Alfred Nobel, 1833. Major-General Sir Ernest Swinton, 1868.

22nd Franz Liszt, 1811. Sarah Bernhardt, 1845. Joan Fontaine, 1917. Jimmy Hanley, 1918.

23rd   Jean Philippe Rameau, 1683. Robert Bridges, 1844. Louis Riel, 1844. George Saintsbury, 1845. Picasso, 1881. Diana Dors, 1931.

24th   Sir Moses Montefiori, 1784. Charles Conder, 1868. Tito Gobbi, 1913.

25th   Elizabeth Farnese, Queen of Spain, 1692. William Wyndham Grenville, Baron Grenville, 1759. Thomas Babington Macaulay, 1800. Johann Strauss the younger, 1825. Rear-Admiral Richard Byrd, 1888. Belita, 1923.

26th   Danton, 1759. Viscount Sankey, 1866. Trotsky, 1879.

27th   Catherine of Valois, 1401. Captain James Cook, 1728. James Macpherson, 1736. Paganini, 1782. Lieut.-General Sir Oliver Leese, 1894.

28th   Erasmus, 1466. Admiral Lord Mountevans, 1881.

29th   James Boswell, 1740. John Keats, 1795. Jean Giraudoux, 1882. Edwige Feuillère, 1907. Frank Sedgman, 1927.

30th   George II, 1683. Andre Marie de Chenier, 1762. Paul Valery, 1871. Ezra Pound, 1885.

31st John Evelyn, 1620. Vermeer, 1632. Pope Clement XIV, 1705. Cosmo Gordon Lang, Baron Lang of Lambeth, 1864. Generalissimo Chiang Kai-shek, 1887. Sir George Hubert Wilkins, 1888. Liddell Hart, 1895.

THE
UPBRINGING
OF OCTOBER
BABIES
OF
THE
PAST

WHEN a child was taken from its mother, and carried outside the bedroom for the first time after its birth, it was lucky to take it *up*stairs, and unlucky to take it *down*stairs. If there were no stairs in the house, the person who carried it generally ascended three steps of a ladder, or temporary erection; and this, it was supposed, would bring prosperity to the child.

Jones, Credulities, 1880.

CHARM FOR CUTTING TEETH. — 'I have made your daughter a present of a wolf's tooth. I sent to Ireland for it, and I set it hear in gold. They ar very Luckey things; for my twoe ferst one did dye, the other bred his very ill, and none of ye Rest did, for I had one for al the rest.' — letter from Lady Wentworth to her son Lord Stafford, March 26th, 1713.

Notes and Queries, 1859.

FOR RUPTURED CHILDREN

An approved powder, by the grace of God, for a child having been ruptured. It has helped many a person already. Take black and white roots of crowfoot, scrape them clean and grind them fine, sift through a sieve. Give every morning before breakfast, in a spoon, while the moon is waning. To an infant only three pinches thereof. Can also be used with advantage by grown persons.

Albertus Magnus, *White and Black Art for Man and Beast*, 13th C.

15 Sept. 1685.

... Very importunate she was that I would sup, and abide there that night, but, being obliged by my companion, I return'd to our inn, after she had shew'd me her house, wch was very commodious and well furnish'd, as she was an excellent housewife, a prudent and virtuous lady. There is a parke full of red deere about it. Her eldest son and other of her children run about, and among the infected, wch she said she let them do on purpose, that they might whilst young pass that fatal disease, which she fancied they were to undergo one time or other, and that this would be the best.

Diary of John Evelyn, Esq.

ROASTED MOUSE. — I have often heard my father say, that when he had the measles, his nurse gave him a roasted mouse to cure him.

SCOTUS.
Notes and Queries, 1850.

. . . Nurses who are fond of medicine are always to be suspected; they trust to it, and neglect their duty, and imagine that medicine will make up for all deficiencies of food, air, exercise, and cleanliness. Where a parent finds her child always asleep, it is advisable that she should remove her child or change her nurse without delay.

A Hand-Book of Domestic Medicine, London: 1855.

It is the custom in Northumberland to make the chrisom-child sleep the first night in the cap he wore at baptism. 'Loud-murmurs,' says my friend, 'arose against me early in my ministerial life for applying so much water that the cap had to be taken off and dried, whereas it should be left on till the next morning. I threw the blame on the modern caps, with their expanse of frilling, on which the good woman said that I was quite right; she had an old christening cap, the heirloom of a friend, which she could show me, of a very different make. Accordingly I examined the cap, which was evidently very old, and made with reference to affusion in baptism. It excluded forehead, ears, and chin, and apparently never had strings. I said that if a mother would bring her baby in such a cap I would undertake not to wet it.'

Henderson, *Folk-Lore of the Northern Counties*, 1879.

CURE FOR THE HOOPING-COUGH. — A farmer, from the neighbourhood of Reepham, in Norfolk, gravely told me the following certain cure for the hooping-cough. Whenever any of his children were attacked with it, he caught a common house-spider, which he tied up in muslin, and pinned over the mantel piece. So long as the spider lived, the cough remained; but when it died the cough went away. He assured me he had cured all his children in this way; and that when two were affected at the same time, they recovered when their respective spiders died, which was not in the order in which they were attacked.

A Correspondent,
Notes and Queries, 1856.

From the Wardrobe Accounts of King Edward IV in the year 1480, for Richard of Shrewsbury Duke of York at the age of 8: ... v yerdes of purpulle velvet for a gowne; v yerdes of grene velvet for a gowne; iii yerdes di' of grene damask for a gowne; a yerde di' of grene satyn; ii yerdes di' of tawny sarsinet, and v yerdes of white cloth of gold for a gowne ...

... In those days, the sons were bred up to learning by terrible discipline: Every Greek and Latin author they conversed with was attended with one or many new scourges, to drive them into acquaintance with him; and not the least misdemeanor in life could escape the lash: As though the father would prove his

daily *love to his son* by never *sparing his rod;* Prov.
xiii. 24. Now-a-days young master must be
treated with a foolish fondness, till he is
grown to the size of man; and let his faults be
never so heinous, and his obstinacy never so
great, yet the preceptor must not let him hear
the name of the rod, lest the child should be
frighted or hurt . . .

In that day, many children were kept in a
most servile subjection, and not suffered to
sit down, or to speak, in the presence of
their father, till they were come to the age of
one-and-twenty. The least degree of freedom
was esteemed a bold presumption, and
incurred a sharp reproof. Now they are
made familiar companions to their parents,
almost from the very nursery; and therefore
they will hardly bear a check or reproof at
their hand.

Isaac Watts, 1674–1748.

FROM THE STATUTE-BOOK: A.D. 1388.

Item. It is ordained & assented, That he
or she which used to labour at the Plough
and Cart, or other Labour or Service of

Husbandry *till they be of the Age of Twelve Years,*
that from thenceforth they shall abide at the same Labour,
without being put to any Mystery or
Handicraft; and if any Covenant or Bond of
Apprentie (*so*) be from henceforth made to
the Contrary, the same shall be holden for
none.

When the days are light enough, the first
class of girls may remain till half-past four
to learn sewing, and the boys knitting. The
teacher reading some story to them while
they are at work. When the days are too
short for this, time for sewing and knitting
must be taken from something else. It is
very desirable that the boys should learn to
knit.

> *A Hand-Book for Teachers of Infant Schools,*
> Manchester and London: 1869.

As we wander along the New Cut during
the day, we do not see so many young
thieves loitering about; but in the evening
when the lamps are lit, they steal forth from
their haunts, with keen roguish eye, looking
out for booty. We then see them loitering

about the stalls or mingling among the throng of people in the street, looking wistfully on the tempting fruit displayed on the stalls.

These young city-dwellers have a very strange and motley appearance. Many of them are only 6 or 7 years of age, others 8 or 10. Some have no jacket, cap, or shoes, and wander about London with their ragged trowsers hung by one brace; some have an old tattered coat, much too large for them, without shoes and stockings, and with one leg of the trowsers rolled up to the knee; others have on an old jacket rent at the elbows, and strips of the lining hanging down behind; others have on an old dirty pinafore; while some have petticoats. They are generally in a squalid and unwashed condition, with their hair clustered in wild disorder like a mop, or hanging down in dishevelled locks, – in some cases cropped close to the head.

Groups of these ragged urchins may be seen standing at the corners of the streets and in public thoroughfares, with blacking-boxes slung on their back by a leathern belt, or crouching in groups on the pavement; or we may occasionally see them running alongside of omnibuses, cabs, and hansoms, nimbly turning somersaults on the pavement as they scamper along, and occasionally walking on their hands with their feet in the air in our fashionable streets, to the merriment of the passers-by. They are generally very acute and ready-witted, and have a knowing twinkle in their eye which exhibits the precocity of their minds . . .

. . . They seldom steal from coster-mongers, but frequently from the old women's stalls. One will push an old woman off her seat – perhaps a bushel basket, while the others will steal her fruit or the few coppers lying on her stall. This is done by day as well as by night, but chiefly in the dusk of evening.

They generally go in a party of three or four, sometimes as many as eight together. Watching their opportunity, they make a sudden snatch at the apples or pears, or oranges or nuts, or walnuts, as the case may be, then run off, with the cry of 'stop thief!'

ringing in their ears from the passers-by.
These petty thefts are often done from a love
of mischief rather than from a desire for
plunder.

Mayhew,
London Labour and the London Poor, 1862.

ROYAL
OCTOBER
BABIES

born October 1773.

Livri, Saturday,
5 August 1786.

I HAVE no fault, my child, to find with you today. You have been uniformly gentle, diligent, and truly amiable. You spoke very well this evening upon the piece of Don Juan; your observations were judicious and proper. It is very pleasing to me to hear you talk with such penetration and good taste – I reminded you at table of something which you said without consideration, and you discovered no ill humour. In general your faults are these: You shew too much heedlessness and indolence; you do not reflect sufficiently; with people of whom you know but little, you are too cold and reserved; and, on the contrary, where you are acquainted and can be at your ease, you are frequently too loquacious; and, lastly, you do not listen enough to what is said by others. You ought to be reminded of these faults, and should accustom yourself to overcome them whenever it is necessary: if you sincerely desire it, you will always succeed. Habituate yourself in like manner to study and understand the characters of those with whom you live: in our conversations you will communicate to me what remarks you may make, and I will give you my sentiments. You should further habituate yourself never to exaggerate any thing, but to represent whatever you may have seen with the most rigid truth. Unless this be your character, you will never be amiable and deserving of esteem.

Sunday, 6 August 1786.

A GOOD day in all respects . . . Observe however that jests and particular expressions are never worth repeating. You were too tedious, for instance, in the jests you bestowed upon my painting. A little raillery, when it is concise and well timed, may be pleasant enough; but if dwelt upon too long, it becomes insipid and troublesome. In your walk you told M—that he was forty-six years old. He does not deny his age; but as he is no longer young, there is no necessity of reminding him of it, particularly in the way of banter; which, in this case, cannot fail to be disagreeable. We should never play our jests on the age of people advanced beyond the meridian of life. I will add to these hints, a tone of conversation somewhat too lofty, and I have nothing more to say: in every thing else my dear child has been good, assiduous and very amiable.

From the Journal of Louis Philippe's
Governess, Madame de Sillery-Brulart,
(formerly Countess de Genlis).

ANOTHER ROYAL OCTOBER BABY

SOPHIA, ELECTRESS OF HANOVER

I was born, they say, on 14th October 1630, and as the twelfth child of the king my father and the queen my mother, I imagine my birth to have afforded them little satisfaction. They were at a loss for a name and godparents for me. All the kings and princes of any importance had already been called into service for the babies born before me.

What was done was to write names on

pieces of paper and leave the choice to chance by drawing for the name; thus I became Sophia. The godmothers of this name found for me were the Princess Palatine de Birckenfeld, Countess of Hohenlohe, the Countess of Culenbourg, and Madame de Brederode, Countess of Nassau; my godfathers were the Estates of Friesland.

I was no sooner transportable than the queen my mother sent me to Leyden, which is only three hours from the Hague. Her Majesty had all her children brought up there away from her, for the sight of her monkeys and dogs was more agreeable to her than that of us.

We had at Leyden a court in the German style. Our schedule was as rigidly prescribed as our curtsies. As my governess, Madame de Ples, had been my father's governess, her age may be imagined. But the two daughters who assisted her looked even older than she did. They were as upright before God as before man. They must have pleased the Former and never bothered the latter. Their aspect was horrible and really adequate to inspire small children with terror. They taught me to love

God and fear the devil, and I was brought up religiously according to the good precepts of Calvin. They taught me the Heidelberg catechism in German, and I knew it all by heart without understanding it. I got up at seven and every morning before getting dressed I had to go to Madamoiselle Marie de Quat, one of the daughters I have mentioned and she had me pray and read the Bible. Then she taught me the verses of Pebrac, at the same time brushing what teeth she had left and rinsing her mouth with grimaces which have remained longer in my imagination than everything she wanted to teach me.

From Sophia's Memoirs.

LADY JANE GREY
born October 1537.

One of the greatest benefits, that ever God gave me, is, that he sent me so sharp and severe Parents, and so gentle a schoolmaster. For when I am in presence either of father or mother, whether I speak, keep silence, sit, stand, or go, eat, drink, be merry, or sad, be sewing, playing, dancing, or doing anything else, I must do it, as it were, in such weight, measure, and number, even so perfectly, as God made the world, or else I am so sharply taunted, so cruelly threatened, yea presently some times, with pinches, nippes, and bobbes, and other ways, which I will not name, for the honor I bear them, so without measure misordered, that I think myself in hell, till time come, that I must go to M. *Elmer*, who teacheth me so gently, so pleasantly, with such fair allurements to learning, that I think all the time nothing whiles I am with him. And when I am called from him, I fall on weeping, because, what soever I do else, but learning, is full of grief, trouble, fear, and whole misliking unto me: And thus my book, hath been so much my pleasure, and bringeth dayly to me more pleasure and more, that in respect of it, all other pleasures, in very deed, be but trifles and troubles to me.

> Lady Jane Grey in a conversation with
> Roger Ascham.

DISTINGUISHED
OCTOBER
BABIES

LORD MACAULAY
born October 1800.

HE himself used to tell a funny story of a nursery scene. For every one who came to his father's house he had a Biblical nickname, Moses, Holofernes, Melchisedek, and the like. One visitor he called 'the Beast'. Kind mamma, prudent papa frowned at their precocious child, and set their brows against his offensive name: but Thomas stuck to his point. Next time the Beast made a morning call, the boy ran to the window which hung over the street; to turn back laughing, crowing with excitement and delight. 'Look here mother,' cries the child, 'you see I am right! Look, look, at the number of the Beast!' Mrs Macaulay glanced at the hackney coach in which her visitor had come, – and behold its number was 666!

Quoted from the *Athenaeum* in
Lord Macaulay, by Henry G. J.
Clements, 1860.

born October 1784.

At Christ-Hospital our dress was of the coarsest and quaintest kind, but was respected out of doors, and is so. It consisted of a blue drugget gown, or body, with ample coats to it; a yellow vest underneath in wintertime; small-clothes of Russia duck; worsted yellow stockings; a leathern girdle; and a little black worsted cap, usually carried in the hand. I believe it was the ordinary dress of children in humble life, during the reign of the Tudors . . .

. . . Our breakfast was bread and water, for the beer was too bad to drink. The bread consisted of the half of a three-halfpenny loaf, according to the prices then current. I suppose it would now be a good twopenny one; certainly not a threepenny. This was not much for growing boys, who had had nothing to eat from six or seven o'clock the preceding evening. For dinner, we had the same quantity of bread, with meat only every other day, and that consisting of a small slice, such as would be given to an infant three or four years old. Yet even that, with all our hunger, we very often left half-eaten; the meat was so tough. On the other days, we had a milk-porridge, ludicrously thin; or rice-milk, which was better. There were no vegetables or puddings. Once a month we had roast beef; and twice a year (I blush to think of the eagerness with which it was looked for!) a dinner of pork. One was roast, and the other boiled; and on the latter occasion we had our only pudding, which was of peas. I blush to remember this, not on account of our poverty, but on account of the sordidness of the custom. There had much better have been none. For supper, we had a like piece of bread, with butter or cheese; and then to bed, with what appetite we might.

Our routine of life was this. We rose to the call of a bell, at six in summer, and seven in winter; and after combing ourselves, and washing our hands and faces, went at the call of another bell to breakfast. All this took up about an hour. From breakfast we proceeded to school, where we remained till eleven, winter and summer, and then had an hour's play. Dinner took place at twelve. Afterwards was a little play till one, when we again went to school, and remained till five in summer and four in winter. At six was the supper. We used to play after it in summer till eight. In winter, we proceeded from supper to bed.

The Autobiography of Leigh Hunt, 1850.

SAMUEL TAYLOR COLERIDGE
born October 1772.

From October 1775 to October 1778. – These three years I continued at the Reading School, because I was too little to be trusted among my Father's schoolboys. After breakfast I had a halfpenny given me, with which I bought three cakes at the baker's shop close by the school of my old mistress; and these were my dinner every day except Saturday and Sunday, when I used to dine at home, and wallowed in a beef and pudding dinner. I am remarkably fond of beans and bacon: and this fondness I attribute to my Father's giving me a penny for having eaten a large quantity of beans on Saturday. For the other boys did not like them, and, as it was an economic food, my Father thought my attachment to it ought to be encouraged. He was very fond of me, and I was my Mother's darling: in consequence whereof I was very miserable. For Molly, who had nursed my brother Francis, and was immoderately fond of him, hated me because my Mother took more notice of me than of Frank; and Frank hated me because my Mother gave me now and then a bit of cake when he had none, – quite forgetting that for one bit of cake which I had and he had not, he had twenty sops in the pan, and pieces of bread and butter with sugar on them from Molly, from whom I received only thumps and ill names.

So I became fretful, and timorous, and a

tell-tale; and the schoolboys drove me from play, and were always tormenting me. And hence I took no pleasure in boyish sports, but read incessantly. I read through all gilt-cover little books that could be had at that time, and likewise all the uncovered tales of Tom Hicka-thrift, Jack the Giant Killer, and the like. And I used to lie by the wall, and mope; and my spirits used to come upon me suddenly, and in a flood; – and then I was accustomed to run up and down the churchyard, and act over again all I had been reading on the docks, the nettles, and the rank grass. At six years of age I remember to have read Belisarius, Robinson Crusoe, and Philip Quarles; and then I found the Arabian Nights' Entertainments, one tale of which, (the tale of a man who was compelled to seek for a pure virgin), made so deep an impression on me, (I had read it in the evening while my mother was at her needle), that I was haunted by spectres, whenever I was in the dark: and I distinctly recollect the anxious and fearful eagerness, with which I used to watch the window where the book lay, and when the sun came upon it, I would seize it, carry it by the wall, and bask, and read. My father found out the effect which these books had produced, and burned them.

S. T. Coleridge,
Biographia Literaria, 1847.

GAMES
for the
OCTOBER
BABY

A FINGER-GAME

DANCE thumbkin, dance!
Dance thumbkin, dance!
(moving the thumb).
Dance ye merry men every one
(moving all the fingers).
For why should thumbkin dance alone?
And so with the fingers in turn, which are
named Foreman, Middleman, Ringman, and
Littleman respectively.

Jackson, *Shropshire Folk-Lore*, 1883.

There must be a leader, and all the rest of the party must sit in a circle. The leader then enters the circle, and says, 'My Granny sent me to you, to work with one, as I do,' working away at the same time with one hand. All instantly then do the same. After a time she cries, 'Stop,' and turning round she says, 'My Granny sent me to you, to work with two, as I do.' All, then, work away with both hands. Next she says, 'to work with three, as I do'; all work with both hands and a foot. Then, 'to work with four, as I do.' That is, with both hands and both feet. Lastly she says, 'to work with all, as I do.' This is the climax. Hands and elbows, legs and head, are all shaking together as rapidly as possible, till want of breath compels them to stop.

Kingston, *Infant Amusements*, 1867.

DUCKING FOR APPLES

... the grand sport with apples on Halloween, is to set them afloat in a tub of water, into which the juveniles, by turns, duck their heads with the view of catching an apple. Great fun goes on in watching the attempts of the youngster in the pursuit of the swimming fruit, which wriggles from side to side of the tub, and evades all attempts to capture it; whilst the disappointed aspirant is obliged to abandon the chase in favour of another whose turn has now arrived. The apples provided with stalks are generally caught first, and then comes the tug of war to win those which possess no such appendages. Some competitors will deftly *suck up* the apple, if a small one, into their mouths. Others plunge manfully overhead in pursuit of a particular apple, and having forced it to the bottom of the tub, seize it firmly with their teeth, and emerge, dripping and triumphant, with their prize. This venturous procedure is generally rewarded with a hurrah! by the lookers-on, and is recommended, by those versed in Halloween-aquatics, as the only sure method of attaining success.

Chambers, Book of Days, 1883.

AN
OCTOBER
CHILD IN
FICTION

A FAMILY of ten children will be always called a fine family, where there are heads and arms and legs enough for the number; but the Morlands had little other right to the word, for they were in general very plain, and Catherine, for many years of her life, as plain as any. She had a thin awkward figure, a sallow skin without colour, dark lank hair, and strong features; – so much for her person; – and not less unpropitious for heroism seemed her mind. She was fond of all boys' plays, and greatly preferred cricket not merely to dolls, but to the more heroic enjoyments of infancy, nursing a dormouse, feeding a canary-bird, or watering a rosebush. Indeed she had no taste for a garden; and if she gathered flowers at all, it was chiefly for the pleasure of mischief – at least so it was conjectured from her always preferring those which she was forbidden to take. – Such were her propensities – her abilities were quite as extraordinary. She never could learn or understand any thing before she was taught; and sometimes not even then, for she was often inattentive, and occasionally stupid. Her mother was three months in teaching her only to repeat the 'Beggar's Petition'; and after all, her next sister, Sally, could say it better than she did. Not that Catherine was always stupid, – by no means; she learnt the fable of 'The Hare and many Friends', as quickly as any girl in England. Her mother wished her to learn music; and Catherine was sure she should like it, for she was very fond of tinkling the keys of the old forlorn spinnet; so, at eight years old she began. She learnt a year, and could not bear it; – and Mrs Morland, who did not insist on her daughters being accomplished in spite of incapacity or distaste, allowed her to leave off. The day which dismissed the music-master was one of the happiest of Catherine's life. Her taste for drawing was not superior; though whenever she could obtain the outside of a letter from her mother, or seize upon any other odd piece of paper, she did what she could in that way, by drawing houses and trees, hens and chickens, all very much like one another. – Writing and accounts she was taught by her father; French by her mother: her proficiency in either was not remarkable, and she shirked her lessons in both whenever she could. What a strange, unaccountable character! – for with all these symptoms of profligacy at ten years old, she had neither a bad heart nor a bad temper; was seldom stubborn, scarcely ever quarrelsome, and very kind to the little ones, with few interruptions of tyranny; she was moreover noisy and wild, hated confinement and cleanliness, and loved nothing so well in the world as rolling down the green slope at the back of the house.

Jane Austen, *Northanger Abbey*, 1818.

LETTERS
from
TWO ROYAL
OCTOBER
CHILDREN

TO you, O king most noble and father most honoured, I owe exceeding thanks; because you have treated me so kindly, like a most loving father, and one who would wish me always to act rightly. I also thank you that you have given me great and costly gifts, as chains, rings, jewelled buttons, neck-chains, and breast-pins, and necklaces, garments, and very many other things; in which things and gifts is conspicuous your fatherly affection towards me; for, if you did not love me, you would not give me these fine gifts of jewellery.

However, you grant me all these, not that I should be proud, and think too much of myself, and fancy I excel others; but that you might urge me to the pursuit of all true virtue and piety, and adorn and finish me with all the accomplishments which are fitting a prince: in short, that I might feel as great love towards you, as you have towards me; which if I did not, I should be ungrateful indeed. For God commandeth me to love my enemy, and how much more to love my father, who brought me into this world.

Farewell, most noble kind and reverend father, and I pray God to keep you.

4th August, 1546.

Edward the Prince.

(Edward VI born October, 1537).
Translation from the Latin as printed in Halliwell, *Letters of the Kings of England*, 1848.

To the Right Honourable and my singular good lord, the Lord-Admiral, give these.

My duty to your lordship, in most humble wise remembered, with no less thanks for the gentle letters which I received from you. Thinking myself so much bound to your lordship for your great goodness towards me from time to time, that I cannot by any means be able to recompense the least part thereof, I purposed to write a few rude lines unto your lordship, rather as a token to show how much worthier I think your lordship's goodness, than to give worthy thanks for the same; and these my letters shall be to testify unto you that, like as you have become towards me a loving and kind father, so I shall be always most ready to obey your godly monitions and good instructions, as becometh one upon whom you have heaped so many benefits. And thus fearing I should trouble your lordship too much, I most humbly take my leave of your good lordship.

Your humble servant during my life,
JANE GRAYE.

(born October 1537)
Letter endorsed at the time:
My Lady Jane, the 1st of Oct., 1548.
Strickland,
Lives of the Tudor Princesses, 1868.

LETTERS
from
OCTOBER
CHILDREN

My Dear Aunt, – as Mr Bird is going to Lichfield on Saturday, I will now take the liberty of writing a few lines to you. I have sent you some flower-seeds, which I hope you will accept, as they are the first-fruits of my garden. I have got coming up three hyacinths, four crocuses, four snowdrops, two tulips, and some more crocuses in a pot. Over the seed that is called convolvulus major you must place a long stick, and the plant will adhere to it and crawl up it. The convolvulus minor will grow to a bush of itself. All the lupins had better be tied up to a stick. Yesterday I planted peas, and to-day beans. I have got a green-and-blue tulip in my garden. I have sent you a plan of my father's house and garden. I sleep in a room by myself, and have done for half a year nearly, and have got a drawer for my playthings, a drawer for my clothes, a washing-stand, a large bed, a chest of drawers, a little red box to keep seeds in with two bottoms, half a dozen pillboxes, a large box to keep my books in, and pens and slate, some silk-worms' eggs, an Ovid's Epistles of Heroes in Latin, which I am learning, Cornelius Nepos, Clarke, and a large Bible which my father gave me. Please to give my love to my uncle, and tell him I am going to send him a line. Believe me, my dear aunt,

You affectionate and dutiful nephew.
Henry Alford D.D., born October 1810.
Life, Journals and Letters,
edited by his widow, 1873.

THOMAS LOVE PEACOCK
born October 1785.

In February, 1795 he wrote a letter which began thus:

Dear Mother, I attempt to write to you a letter
In verse, tho' in prose I could do it much better;

The Muse, this cold weather, sleeps up at
    Parnassus,
And leaves us poor poets as stupid as asses:
She'll tarry still longer, if she has a warm
    chamber,
A store of old massie, ambrosia, and amber.
Dear mother, don't laugh, you may think she
    is tipsy,
And I, if a poet, must drink like a gipsy.

    . . . continued for 24 lines more, and ended
thus:

  The bard craves one shilling of his own
    dear mother,
And, if you think proper, add to it another.

RHYMES
for the
OCTOBER
BABY

B ROWN October brings the
pheasant,
Then to gather nuts is pleasant.
　　　　Sara Coleridge (1802–1852).

A distinguished Logician of Fife
Rode out every day of his life,
On a cream-coloured cow,
And this conduct somehow
He found was productive of strife.
His neighbours, who long had felt sad-ish,
Believed the Logician was mad-ish;
But he said: 'To be brief,
I shall ride my own beef,
Till I manage to find a horse-radish.'
New Comical Nursery Rhymes and Funny Stories,
　　　　　　　　　　London, 1866.

　　Two little dogs
　　　Sat by the fire
　　Over a fender of coal-dust;
　　　Said one little dog

80

To the other little dog,
If you don't talk, why I must.
Nursery Rhymes, Tales and Jingles,
London, 1844.

What's the news of the day,
Good neighbour, I pray?
They say the balloon
Is gone up to the moon.
Nursery Rhymes of England,
collected by Halliwell, 1843.

There was a Young Person of Crete,
Whose toilette was far from complete;
She dressed in a sack, spickle-speckled with
black,
That ombliferous person of Crete.
Edward Lear (1812–1888).

LULLABY

Hushie ba, burdie beeton!
Your mammie's gane to Seaton,
For to buy a lammie's skin,
To wrap your bonnie boukie in.
Popular Rhymes of Scotland,
W. & R. Chambers, 1842.

A CHILD'S EVENING PRAYER

Ere on my bed my limbs I lay,
God grant me grace my prayers to say:
O God! preserve my mother dear
In health and strength for many a year;
And, O! preserve my father too,
And may I pay him reverence due;
And may I my best thoughts employ
To be my parents' hope and joy;
And O! preserve my brothers both
From evil doings and from sloth,
And may we always love each other,
Our friends, our father, and our mother:
And still, O Lord, to me impart,
An innocent and grateful heart,
That after my great sleep I may
Awake to thy eternal day!

Amen.

S. T. Coleridge (1772–1832).

GOODNIGHT
to the
OCTOBER
BABY

WHETHER you live in the town or in the country, it is likely someone is burning leaves, so the lovely bonfire tang is blown into your room. A bonfire smell is perhaps the most nostalgic of all smells. It brings back to everybody their childhood when they stood intoxicated, watching the sparks fly, or wild with excitement danced round the flames, or perhaps were allowed to roast potatoes in the ashes. It belongs to the time when nothing was impossible, when anything could happen.

Suppose you could go back, probably only a few years, to the days when you believed anything was possible, even the arrival of a fairy godmother, or a genie who could give you three wishes for your baby, for what would you wish? Would you like the traditional health, wealth and happiness, or would you choose something special? Do you long for a son who becomes a prime minister, or a millionaire? Would you like a daughter who would grow up to be a Margot Fonteyn, or a film star? It is a sobering thought that when you were a baby your mother too might have been granted three wishes, and to speculate what she would have wished for you. How would you have turned out if she had? Would you have been as happy as, at this minute, you are? It is lucky, really, that wishes belong to childhood, for the temptation to use them if they were given would be so enormous, and such a mistake, for really you know in your heart you love your baby just the way it is.

Noel Streatfeild